Amazing Animals
Rainforest Romp

KINGFISHER
LONDON & NEW YORK

Text copyright © 2009 by Tony Mitton
Illustrations copyright © 2009 by Ant Parker
Consultancy by David Burnie

Published in the United States by Kingfisher,
175 Fifth Ave., New York, NY 10010
Kingfisher is an imprint of Macmillan Children's Books, London.
All rights reserved.

Distributed in the U.S. by Macmillan, 175 Fifth Ave., New York, NY 10010
Distributed in Canada by H.B. Fenn and Company Ltd., 34 Nixon Road, Bolton, Ontario L7E 1W2

Library of Congress Cataloging-in-Publication Data
has been applied for.

ISBN: 978-0-7534-6298-0

Kingfisher books are available for special promotions and premiums. For details contact:
Special Markets Department, Macmillan, 175 Fifth Avenue, New York, NY 10010.

For more information, please visit www.kingfisherpublications.com

First American Edition August 2009
Printed in China
2 4 6 8 10 9 7 5 3

To Jasmine & Freya in Derbyshire—T. M.
For Geoff and Graham—A. P.

Amazing Animals
Rainforest Romp

Tony Mitton and Ant Parker

KINGFISHER
NEW YORK

In South American forests,
the trees grow thick and tall.

So many creatures live there,
it's hard to count them all.

The tapir is a mammal.
It's hoofed and rather stout.

It sniffs for tasty plant life
with its clever, stretchy snout.

The giant armadillo has skin
like armored scales.

Whatever wants to munch it
just hurts its teeth and fails.

A jaguar's a great big cat that climbs and stalks and swims.

It prowls around for jungle
prey on stealthy, silent limbs.

This snake's an anaconda.
Be careful of it, please.

Don't let it try to cuddle you.
It just might start to squeeze.

Beware the poisonous tree frog.
Although it's cute to see,

its color is a warning
that tells us, "Let me be!"

These big-billed birds are toucans.
They like to live in twos.

For eating fruit and insects,
those bills are good to use.

A sloth moves very slowly.
How shy it seems to be.

It likes to live alone and hardly
ever leaves its tree.

Here are howler monkeys.
They hang around up high.

From far across the forest
you'll hear them as they cry.

Our rainforest romp is over.
Didn't we see a lot?

Toucans, frogs, and prowling cats—
but what else did you spot?

Did you spot . . .

the agouti?

the golden cock-of-the-rock?

the emerald tree boa?

the silky anteater?

the spider monkey?

the golden lion tamarin?

the uakari monkey?

the capybara?

the hoatzin?